HELENSBUR
ROSNEATH I
INCLUDING CARDROS
& LOCH L

THE GUIDE BOOK

First published in 2013
by
Aird Trading (Publishing)
www.scotlandbooks.co.uk
www.scotlandguidebooks.co.uk

Authors: Lynne Woods & Doug Vickers

ISBN 978-0-9562126-7-2

over Picture: Henry Bell's Comet Flywheel, East Esplanade, Helensburgh

INTRODUCTION

Welcome to "Helensburgh & The Rosneath Peninsula" (including Cardross, Garelochhead and Loch Long), another in the series "See it....Do it....Don't Miss It....". The aim of each of these books is to help the visitor to do just that; to make the most of their stay in a given area.

This particular area is the gateway to the Cowal Peninsula. However, it has much to offer as a destination in its own right and is well worth time spent exploring. Helensburgh is a lively, bustling town, whilst its environs provide a quieter, tranquil setting for those wishing to take life at a more leisurely pace. This book ends just south of Arrochar, which is included in another of the "See it, Do it, Don't Miss It...." series - "Cowal & Bute: The Guide Book". The area to the east of Arrochar is covered in "Loch Lomond & The Trossachs: The Guide Book".

The purpose of these guides is to point out the major attractions but also to encourage you to explore "off the beaten track" and discover places you might otherwise not find. Because all our books are checked by local people before publication, we hope to provide an accurate picture of what is to be seen as well as the chance to discover some of Scotland's lesser known delights.

The book is arranged in a logical order for touring the area, as shown by the map on page 4. Please note that the map is not intended for precise navigation – its purpose is to indicate the general location of things mentioned in the text. An index of place names for easy reference is included on page 22. A list of useful telephone numbers can be found on page 23.

Public toilets are not generally listed as many of these have been closed in recent years. In some places, village halls have made their facilities available. Elsewhere "comfort partnerships" have been agreed with hotels who make their toilets available to non-patrons – look out for signs.

Whilst every effort has been made to ensure accuracy, things do change with the creation of new enterprises and the disappearance of others as people retire or move on, a fact for which the publishers cannot accept responsibility.

If this is the first time you have followed one of our guide books we hope that it will enable you to make the most of your time in and around Helensburgh, Rosneath Gareloch & Loch Long and that it creates a wish to return soon or to use one of our other books to explore a different area.

CONTENTS

4. Area Map

5. Helensburgh

11. Ardmore, Geilston & Cardross

14. Gareloch and Garelochhead

17. The Rosneath Peninsula

21. Loch Long

22. Index

23. Helensburgh Heritage Room
Useful Telephone Numbers
Acknowledgements

24. See it, Do it, Don't Miss it: The series

Highland Cattle on The Ardardan Estate

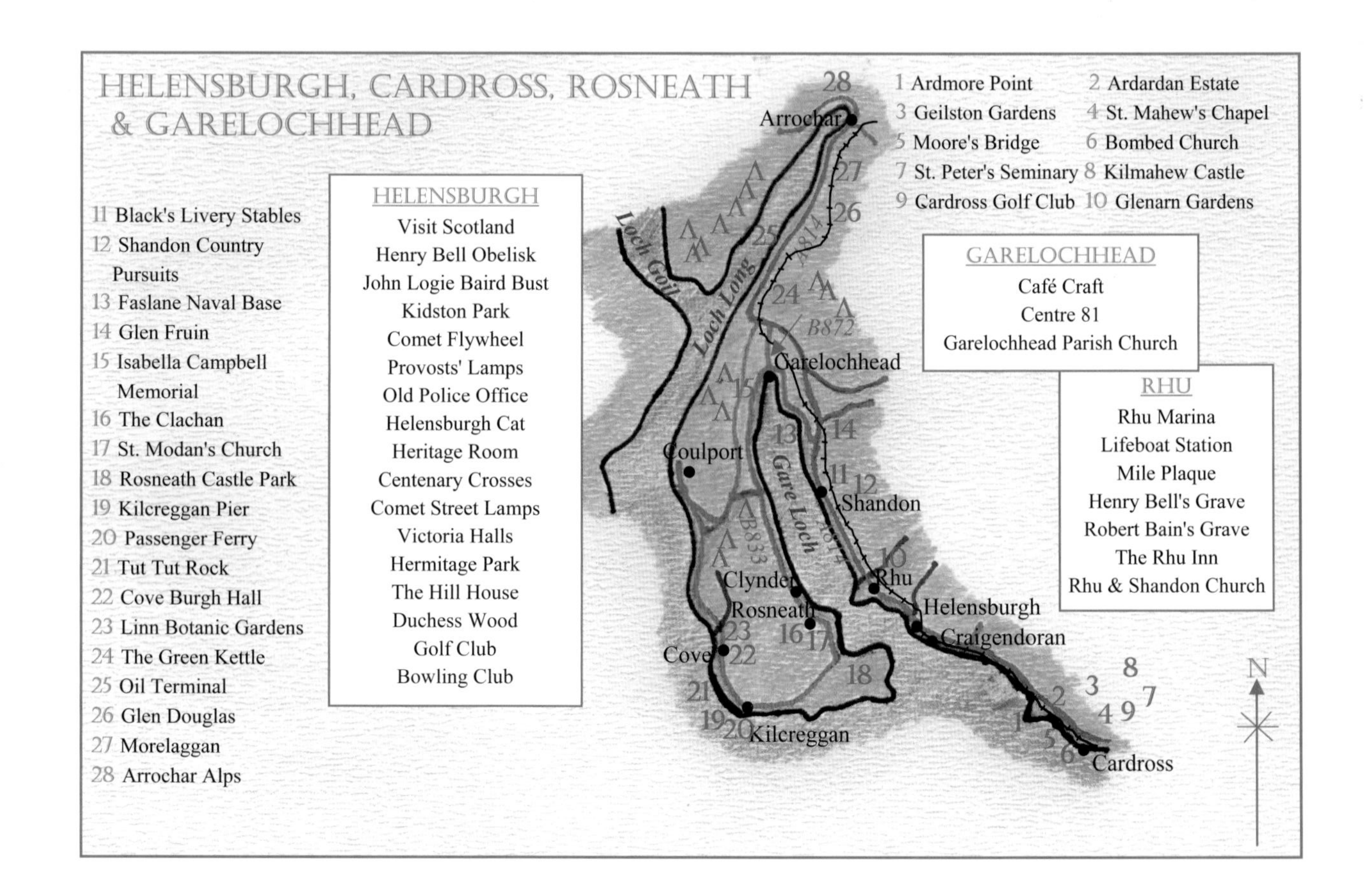
HELENSBURGH, CARDROSS, ROSNEATH & GARELOCHHEAD
11 Black's Livery Stables
12 Shandon Country Pursuits
13 Faslane Naval Base
14 Glen Fruin
15 Isabella Campbell Memorial
16 The Clachan
17 St. Modan's Church
18 Rosneath Castle Park
19 Kilcreggan Pier
20 Passenger Ferry
21 Tut Tut Rock
22 Cove Burgh Hall
23 Linn Botanic Gardens
24 The Green Kettle
25 Oil Terminal
26 Glen Douglas
27 Morelaggan
28 Arrochar Alps
HELENSBURGH
Visit Scotland
Henry Bell Obelisk
John Logie Baird Bust
Kidston Park
Comet Flywheel
Provosts' Lamps
Old Police Office
Helensburgh Cat
Heritage Room
Centenary Crosses
Comet Street Lamps
Victoria Halls
Hermitage Park
The Hill House
Duchess Wood
Golf Club
Bowling Club
1 Ardmore Point
2 Ardardan Estate
3 Geilston Gardens
4 St. Mahew's Chapel
5 Moore's Bridge
6 Bombed Church
7 St. Peter's Seminary
8 Kilmahew Castle
9 Cardross Golf Club
10 Glenarn Gardens
GARELOCHHEAD
Café Craft
Centre 81
Garelochhead Parish Church
RHU
Rhu Marina
Lifeboat Station
Mile Plaque
Henry Bell's Grave
Robert Bain's Grave
The Rhu Inn
Rhu & Shandon Church
Arrochar
Loch Goil
Loch Long
A814
B872
Garelochhead
Coulport
Gare Loch
Shandon
B833
Clynder
Rosneath
Rhu
Helensburgh
Craigendoran
Cove
Kilcreggan
Cardross
N

Provost's Lamp

Helensburgh is an elegant town "with its many fine houses and fair gardens set on the hillside...." (J.J.Bell: The Glory of Scotland 1932.) The A818 from Loch Lomond provides a dramatic entrance, with magnificent views over the rooftops to the Clyde and beyond. On the opposite bank of the river are Greenock and Gourock, whose development have been fundamental to Helensburgh's own prosperity.

Situated where the Gareloch meets the Clyde, the town was largely built by Sir James Colquhoun as an 18th century spar resort, with baths beside the old Ardencaple Castle. He named the new town after his wife Helen. Establishment of a steamer ferry service between Helensburgh and Gourock ensured a growing population of those who became wealthy from Clyde industries, such as ship building and sugar refining. Many spacious villas can be seen around the town.

In 1808 the baths and a hotel were bought by Henry Bell (see page 6) who, in 1812, built the paddle steamer "Comet" - the first commercially successful steamboat in Europe. As more steamers appeared on the Clyde, the town became a popular destination for holidays and day trips. In 1858, the Glasgow, Dumbarton and Helensburgh Railway arrived, then in 1894 the West Highland Railway to Fort William, making the town even more accessible.

Sinclair Street

Modern Helensburgh is still a popular holiday destination and home to many people working in Glasgow or at the nearby Faslane Naval Base. The last remaining sea-going paddle steamer, Waverley, still calls here during the summer.

John Logie Baird, inventor of the television, (see page 7) was a notable Helensburgh-born personality, as was actress Deborah Kerr and entertainer Jack Buchanan who was a lifelong friend of Baird.

The West Esplanade

The West Esplanade has a large car park, which sensibly charges for 15 minute slots. (The sea end of the car park is free!) Nearby is the pier, a swimming pool, fairground and tourist information. Until 2012 a ferry crossed the Clyde from here. The wide promenade has well kept lawns and flower beds, palm trees, a cycle lane and some interesting memorials. Opposite are hops, restaurants and cafés, above which much of the older Victorian architecture can e seen. The Clyde Sea Lochs Trail begins here.

'isit Scotland has an information office (seasonal) adjacent to the car park and oused in an interesting tower, the remains of a former church.

The Imperial Hotel retains two ornate lamps from a bygone era although closer inspection reveals their twenty-first century low energy light bulbs!
Henry Bell Obelisk: A large, granite obelisk, erected in 1872, commemorates Henry Bell "the first in Great Britain who was successful in practically applying steam power to the purpose of navigation". (See below.)
Bust of John Logie Baird: This bears the inscription "John Logie Baird, native of this town, inventor of the television. 1888 – 1946. They need no candle". (See page 7.)

Henry Bell (1767 – 1830) became one of Helensburgh's most famous sons. Multi-talented, he trained as both stonemason and millwright, studied ship modelling and worked in London under engineer John Rennie before moving back to Scotland. Throughout this time he pursued an interest in the possibility of using steam power to drive large vessels and corresponded with like-minded engineers worldwide. In 1808, he and his wife moved to Helensburgh. He bought The Baths Hotel which his wife ran while he concentrated on designing. In 1811 he commissioned shipbuilder John Wood to construct a thirty ton paddle steamer with a three horse power engine. "Comet" became the first commercially viable steamer in Europe, operating a ferry service on the Clyde and further afield from 1812 until 1820 when it was wrecked in a storm near Oban. Undaunted, Bell built a second Comet but this was not financially successful.
Bell became the first provost of Helensburgh. He died in 1830. An obelisk on the esplanade honours his memory and a leaflet "The Henry Bell Trail" is available from Visit Scotland or from www.helensburgh-heritage.co.uk. In the library is a model of the first Comet.

Kidston Park, at Cairndhu Point where the Gareloch meets the Clyde, is delightful Gifted to the town by William Kidston of Fernigair in 1877, it has ample parking, a children's playground, bandstand and seats to enjoy the fabulous views.

Sunset from Kidstons

Kidstons is a family orientated café serving reasonably priced, healthy snacks and meals. At night, Kidstons is transformed into a wine bar/café Open: Summer. 09.00 – 22.00. Winter 09.00 – 17.00.
Dino's Café & Ice Cream Parlour is a retro-style diner serving delicious Italian ice cream, made on the premises to the same recipe since 1924.
Rowan Gallery incorporates a design-led gift shop and hosts frequently changing

John Logie Baird (1888 – 1946), inventor of the television, was born in Helensburgh. The son of a minister, he studied electrical engineering at Glasgow's Royal Technical College (now part of Strathclyde University) before moving to Hastings where he worked on developing a method of transmitting moving images using photoelectric cells to scan objects. He produced his first rudimentary television apparatus in 1924. Having proved its viability, the BBC made its first television broadcast in 1936. Although subsequently the method was improved by EMI-Marconi, it was Baird who paved the way and who continued to develop new ideas. In 1944 he was the first person in the world to demonstrate colour television although this was not adopted at the time, due wartime austerity. Baird died in 1946 – a full twenty-three years before colour television finally entered our homes! Along the west seafront is a bust to commemorate his achievements.

John Logie Baird

exhibitions of work by contemporary Scottish artists including Pam Carter and Gerard M. Burns.

MacGillivray's Scottish Gifts & Coffee Shop is the place to find silver and gold Celtic jewellery, cuff links and kilt pins, Scottish soaps & biscuits, enjoy a coffee and home made cakes and soup. (The treacle scones are yummy!)

The Commodore Inn is a riverside, country style pub and restaurant with an extensive menu and a selection of award-winning cask ales. Themed nights include the popular "pie night". Live jazz on the first Thursday of the month throughout the year.

The East Esplanade

This land was reclaimed from the sea in the late 19th century. An information board tells of Henry Bell's life and work. A leaflet, "The Henry Bell Trail", is available from Visit Scotland.

The Comet Flywheel

The Comet Flywheel situated on the green is from the original engine of Henry Bell's first "Comet". Beneath is set the anvil used by his blacksmith Daniel McMurrich.

The Queen's Hotel

The Queen's Hotel: A castellated frontage, still bearing the name "Queen's Hotel" and now luxury apartments, was formerly the Baths Inn, built by Henry Bell and managed by his wife.

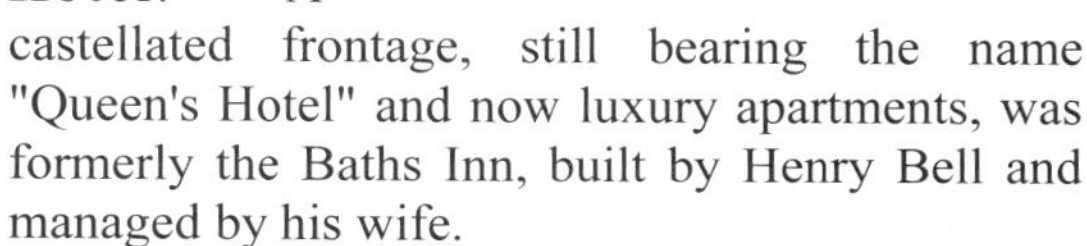

Provosts' Lamps stand in front of the former

Queens Hotel. (A provost is the Scottish equivalent of a mayor.) It was customary to have two lamp posts outside a provost's house to identify it. On leaving office, one of the lamps would be removed. One of these stood outside Henry Bell's house. (See page 6.)

The Town Centre

In the streets behind the sea front are some of the main chain stores and many smaller independent retailers, too numerous to mention all. There are many architecturally interesting buildings, including an unusually large number of churches.

St Columba's Church: The tall square tower of St. Columba's Church dominates the skyline. Erected in 1861 to a design by William Spence, it was originally the United Secession Church, of which Henry Bell's wife was an early member. The last service here was held in 2011, prior to the congregation joining with that of West Kirk in Colquhoun Square to become St. Andrew's Kirk.

The Old Police Office and Court on Sinclair Street is a striking example of 19th century Scottish Baronial architecture with ornate castellation. The court building, now municipal offices, was designed in 1878 by renowned Scottish architect John Honeyman. With the arrival of the railway, the building was extended to incorporate the station and, in 1906, extended further by local architect A. N. Paterson to include the police office and fire station.

The Helensburgh Cat

The Helensburgh Cat is a sculpture high (near the drainpipe) on the former police office on Sinclair Street. During construction a cat arrived each day to be fed by the workmen, who grew fond of it. Paterson incorporated it into the building.

Quirky Sculptures: Two figures can be spotted on a first storey windowsill above one of the shops on Sinclair Street (in the block between East Clyde Street and East Princes Street). There is also a statue of St Andrew on the façade and, above a nearby window, the tree of life.

Bust of Henry Bell: Over the main door of the municipal buildings on East Princes Street is a sculpted bust of Henry Bell.

Callaghan's Fine Foods is the place to sample authentic Scottish food. A family run butchers, selling Scottish meat and game, Callaghan's produce their own extra rich haggis, famous steak pies and venison burgers. A speciality is home-made black pudding embedded in Scottish lorne. (Lorne is traditional Scottish square, sliced sausagemeat.)

The Heritage Centre in the library contains an original Logie Baird "televisor" as well as a working model, distributed as a kit with The Daily Express in the 1920's. Before the days of TV, this demonstrated the basic principal of transmitting images

Other displays include the role of steamers in the town's development and information about film star Deborah Kerr, born in the town in 1921, and entertainer Jack Buchanan.

The Church of St. Michael & All Angels at the corner of West Princes Street and William Street, is beautiful. It has been extensively restored. It was designed in the Gothic Style by Sir Robert Rowand Anderson and completed in 1868, William Gladstone contributing to the cost. Most striking is its vivid interior, including an exceptional collection of stained glass. The reredos (altar back) is a colourful alabaster and glass mosaic of the crucifixion. Behind are beautiful geometric mosaic tiles depicting the seven gifts of the Holy Spirit. (One tile is upside down – the Victorians often incorporated imperfections to acknowledge that only God is perfect.) Above the organ pipes are two carved angels. The pulpit, unusually, is also made of alabaster. Visitors welcome.

St. Michael & All Angels

St. Michael & All Angels

Colquhoun Square

At the bustling intersection of Colquhoun Street and West Princes Street, the square has attractive flower beds, a lovely Victorian post office, St. Andrew's Kirk, quirky street lamps and several memorials.

Colquhoun Square

Centenary Crosses: Two Celtic crosses commemorate the 1902 and 2002 centenaries of Helensburgh's burgh charter.

Comet Street Lamps: Easy to miss, unless you are looking for them, are the likenesses of Comet which feature on the street lamps here.

St. Andrew's Kirk, originally The West United Free Church, was designed by James Hay in 1845. The porch, by renowned architect Leiper, was added in 1892. The interior dates from later, due to a fire in 1924 in which all but the walls were destroyed. The unusual timber ceiling, a trade mark of Hay's, was faithfully reproduced after the fire. The church later became St. Andrew's Church of Scotland, then the West Kirk, and now St. Andrew's Kirk. The oak panelling was brought to the church relatively recently from St. Bride's Church prior to that building's demolition in 1993 when the two congregations joined together.

East King Street

East King Street is a must for anyone interested in church architecture. Within the space of a few hundred yards are three lovely old churches.

Helensburgh Baptist Church is a pretty little church, built in 1886 although a Baptist congregation had been established in Helensburgh some fifty years earlier. The building was used as a refugee centre in WWII for victims of the Clydebank Blitz. A stained glass window commemorates church members who served as missionaries in India. The church is especially welcoming and usually open to visitors.

Park Church was designed in the Gothic style by Honeyman and built in 1862-1863 with later additions by Leiper. It became a parish church in 1929 when The Church of Scotland and The United Free Church amalgamated. It has a particularly intricate rose window and an unusual rectangular belfry crowned by a tall circular spire.

St. Joseph's RC Church, built in 1880, is a beautiful red sandstone building with imposing twin main doors, above which is a lovely statue of St. Joseph. In the grounds is a tableau of the Crucifixion.

Upper Helensburgh

The Victoria Halls is an impressive building erected in 1887 to celebrate Queen Victoria's Golden Jubilee. A sculpture of her is worked into the front of the building. Built as a gathering place, with halls and meeting rooms it serves the same community purpose now as then. It has in recent years been extensively restored. (Note the lovely thistles on the gate of the house next door!)

The Victoria Halls

The Hermitage Park, adjacent to the Victoria Halls, has landscaped grounds and woodland walks. Left neglected, it was in danger of becoming a wilderness until 2011 when The Friends of Hermitage Park began to restore the park to its former glory. The Malig Burn runs through the grounds, once powering a water mill, the ruins of which remain. In summer there are tennis courts, bowling and skateboarding. A War Memorial garden contains a beautiful "A" listed Cenotaph.

Helensburgh Golf Club, originally with only nine holes but now with eighteen and a par 69, was founded in 1893 and enjoys spectacular views over the town. Much of its present layout was influenced by a visit in the 1920s by professional golfer and renowned course designer James Braid. Visiting golfers welcome.

The Hill House

The Hill House is quite simply stunning. Designed by Charles Rennie Mackintosh (1868 – 1928) for publisher Walter Blackie, it was completed in 1903 and is considered to be Mackintosh's finest domestic work and a worldwide example of the best of early 20th century Art Nouveau design. Its greatest surprise is that, over a hundred years later

(Image of The Hill House included with kind permission of The National Trust for Scotland.)

it still looks "modern" today. The house and its contents, to the tiniest detail, are in complete harmony with each other, a truly elegant blend of simplicity and detail. Of particular note is the way natural light has been maximised within the confines of the house. The drawing room is particularly fine. Mackintosh's wife was a talented textile artist, much of the interior showing her influence or worked by her – she designed and executed the antimacassars and the sleeping princess panels above the fireplace. (Replicas now replace the original antimacassars.) The house was designed as a family home, with some lovely humorous touches: Blackie was very fond of roses and of his yacht. Mackintosh stencilled roses on the drawing room walls, one or more petals of which have turned into boats! In the dining room are portraits of Mr. and Mrs. Blackie, she with her fingers entwined while reading a book – something about which she was often teased by the family. The house is now in the care of the National Trust for Scotland. Open: House & shop Apr. 1st to 31st Oct. 13.30. – 17.30. Tea room: 13.30 – 17.00.

Duchess Wood, on the north west outskirts of Helensburgh, is a delightful community woodland of mature trees, burns and bridges and especially renowned for its spring bluebells. A wheelchair and pushchair friendly path runs through part of the woods which are dotted with information boards. Deer frequent the woods and the characteristic tap of the woodpecker's beak is often heard.

ARDMORE, GEILSTON & CARDROSS

From Helensburgh the A814 runs east along the edge of the Clyde towards Dumbarton and Glasgow.

Craigendoran (Gaelic: "Creag an Dobrain" – "rock of the otter") once had a busy pier where North British Railway passengers could connect with steamers for Gourock. The service ended in 1972 and the pier is now derelict.

Ardmore Point: Geological upheaval millions of years ago resulted in unusual rock formations here, including an anticline and a fault line. There is also a cave. Excavations in the 1950s unearthed hearth stones, charcoal, deer bones and pottery from an iron age settlement. Today, it is a popular place for watching widgeon, shelduck, redshank, goosanders and large numbers of oystercatchers as well as osprey and grey seals.

Ardardan Farm Shop

Ardardan Estate has a beautiful walled garden with a tea room serving light lunches and home baking. There are also woodland walks, a plant nursery and an exceptionally tempting food hall selling Scottish produce, including fresh eggs and homebred beef and lamb. Open Tue. – Sun. 10.00 – 17.00.

Geilston Gardens

Geilston Gardens, managed by The National Trust for Scotland, are a delight. Although the late 17th century house is not open to the public, the gardens transport one back to a gentler age with a kitchen garden, glass houses and a peaceful walled garden dominated by a spectacular giant Wellington tree – a coniferous species originating from Calafornia. The new herbaceous borders are planted in the naturalistic style with bold blocks or waves of American prairie species. The potting shed dates from 1797. The 40 foot glasshouse remains much as it would have looked when first erected, considered to be a fine example of the work of Mackenzie and Moncur. By the car park is a small but pleasant sitting area where it is possible to enjoy a good cup of coffee. Plants and fresh vegetables are available to purchase from July to October. Open: Apr. – Oct. 09.30 – 17.00.

(Images of Geilston Gardens included with kind permission of The National Trust for Scotland.)

Cardross:

Cardross is a place of well tended gardens, swept roads and clean bus shelters. The village dates from the 17th century. It was the birth place, in 1896, of A. J. Cronin, whose novel "Country Doctor" became the TV series "Dr. Finlay's Casebook". An earlier notable was Robert the Bruce who built a manor here, where he died in 1329.

St. Mahew's Chapel is a Roman Catholic church on the site of different houses of worship throughout the centuries, the present one dating from the 1400s. Restored in the 1950s, it stands in the area known as Kilmahew, "cill" meaning a church or cell and "Mahew" an early missionary saint. It is a pretty, white painted, low building with a small bell tower. In the vestibule is a stone, carved with a cross, thought to have been etched by St. Mahew. The church, not normally open to the public, has some ancient gravestones in the grounds.

St. Mahew's Chapel

Cardross Parish Church was built in 1872 as The Free Church, becoming the Parish Church after the original one (see page 13) was destroyed by a bomb in May 1941. Notable is its full octave of eight bells, the original five having been added to in 1914 and again at the Millennium. The beautiful interior is especially renowned for its textiles and stained glass windows. Three exquisite embroidered panels, created by textile artist

Hannah Frew Paterson, are mounted behind the altar. The intricate stitching and appliqué work represents the whole of Creation, depicting a hillside as backdrop to the wooden cross above the altar. The four Gospel windows are by John Lawrie DA, formerly head of The Department of Glass Design at Edinburgh University. Symbols of the Gospels are etched in clear plate glass so that light and colours from outside blend with the designs to stunning effect.

The Millennium Bible Garden opposite the church is a peaceful oasis for quiet contemplation.

SWRI Seat

SWRI Seat : A quaint, roofed seat at the end of Station Road was gifted by the Cardross branch of the Scottish Women's Rural Institute in 1932.

The War Memorial on the main road is of a simple art deco design.

Drinking Fountain: Set in the wall adjacent to the War Memorial is a 1918 drinking fountain.

Cardross Golf Course was established over a century ago and the stunning views over the Clyde are hard to equal. It is described as "a testing par 71 course". Like Helensburgh golf course, it was redesigned by James Braid. Professional's shop. Visitors welcome.

The Coach House Inn was once a busy coaching inn. It is now a homely, family run pub serving food (12.00 - 21.00 daily) and real ale. Pool, darts, Wi-Fi, live music on Saturday night and a monthly Sunday jazz afternoon. B and B.

Moore's Bridge on the left, heading east, carries the main road over the Kilmahew Burn. The bridge was widened in the 19th century but incorporates part of the original 1688 bridge. It consists of a painted "clairvoyee" (ironwork fence) with inscriptions on the stones at either side, one bearing a coat of arms and the other the date and the words "Not we but God, Jean Watson". Jean Watson's (married name Moore) generosity paid for the erection of the older bridge. NB: Take care - This is a busy stretch of road and there is no parking on the bridge.

The "Bombed Church" is the remains of the parish church, built in 1827. In May

Moore's Bridge, Cardross

The "Bombed Church"

1941 German bombs destroyed all but its large square tower, which was restored in 1999. In the churchyard are two mausoleums and some ornate gravestones featuring a draped urn, symbolic of the soul and death.

St. Peter's Seminary, hidden away in Kilmahew Forest and now fallen into disrepair, is a remarkable example of post war modernist architecture. Constructed in concrete and with striking lines, it was designed by Gillespie, Kidd and Coia and built as a seminary for trainee priests in the grounds of the elegant 1865 Kilmahew House. (GR354784) Completed in 1966, it was never fully occupied and was abandoned in the 1980s although a charity, assisted by Glasgow University, is working to restore it. Kilmahew House burned down in 1995.

Kilmahew Castle was once the home of the Napiers of Kilmahew but is now in ruins.

GARELOCH AND GARELOCHHEAD

From Helensburgh, the A814 north follows the shoreline, passing several gatehouses - evidence of secluded mansions. Two particularly pretty lodges are those of Dalmore House, now apartments but once the home of a wealthy sugar refiner. A bus service runs alongside Gareloch, which is approximately 10 km/6.2 miles long and extends from Helensburgh, where it joins the Firth of Clyde, to Garelochhead. It is separated from Loch Long to the west by the narrow Rosneath Peninsula. (see page 17) Much of eastern Gareloch is inaccessible due to the presence of the Faslane Naval Base. There is also a large oil terminal on the loch, where crude oil is unloaded and sent fifty miles by pipeline to Grangemouth Refinery.

Rhu

The name derives from the Gaelic "rubha" or "rudha" meaning a point. It is a quaint village with 16th and 17th century cottages and a fascinating graveyard. It was from Rhu that many hundreds of people embarked on the hazardous journey to a new life during the infamous "Clearances". Sailing from Rhu nowadays is a happier event for here is one of the Clyde's main yachting centres, with a large marina. Each New Year's Day hardy souls take a swim in the Clyde from here. During WWII Rhu was the site of the MAEE (Marine Aircraft Experimental Establishment) - a secret arm of The Air Ministry, named RAF Helensburgh, which developed and tested seaplanes and bombs.

The Ardencaple Hotel was a mid 18th century coaching inn and is now a lovely hotel with character and original features. Wheelchair friendly room available. Bar meals served.

Rhu Marina offers full marina facilities and has an RYA training centre, coastguard office and lifeboat station.

Café Rhu, at the marina, serves "fresh and hearty" food between 08.00 and 16.00 daily to eat in or take away. Takeaway fish and chips, Fridays, 17.00 – 20.00.
Helensburgh Lifeboat Station: The Atlantic 21 class RIB (rigid inflatable) called The Andrew Mason carries a crew of three. If capsized it can be righted by activating an air bag on the roll bar and the inversion proof engine, invented by RNLI engineers, can be re-started. (Not generally open to the public.)
Mile Plaque: Opposite the marina is an old fashioned mile plaque with pointing hands giving the distances to Dumbarton (10 miles), Garelochhead (5 ½ miles) and Arrochar (15½ miles).

Glenarn Gardens surround Glenarn House, built in the 1840s. The Gibson family bought it in 1927 and spent fifty years creating the gardens, many plants collected from early foreign expeditions. Since 1983 the Thornley family have restored the gardens, renowned for the collection of rhododendrons, magnolias and rock plants. Leaflet and map available from a dispenser at the entrance. Dogs welcome on a short lead. Donation box near the house. Parking on Glenarn Road. Open daily 21st Mar. – 21st Sep. sunrise - sunset. .

The Rhu Inn, once the haunt of whisky smugglers, was built in the mid 19th century. It occupies the site of the 17th century Colquhoun Arms. It was remodelled in the late 19th and early 20th centuries to include stained glass windows by renowned glass artist Favrile and which features a pattern patented by Tiffany in 1894. Real ale fans can sample the beers of local micro breweries while whisky connoisseurs can enjoy a dram from the extensive range of malts. Live music at weekends.
Rhu & Shandon Parish Church has an unusual Gothic tower resembling a tall crown upon a square base and which contains a bell which chimes on the quarter hour. The church was built by William Spence in 1851 and enlarged by Honeyman and Keppie only forty years later. The ornate nature and elaborate inscriptions on the gravestones are a testimony to the enterprising nature and prosperity of former inhabitants, many having returned from overseas after making their fortunes.
Henry Bell's Grave is marked by a large statue of Bell (1767 – 1830), the stone plinth detailing his achievement in building "the first steam vessel in Europe which successfully navigated rivers and open seas". The statue was erected by Glasgow engineer and ship builder Robert Napier in 1851.

Henry Bell Statue

Robert Bain's Gravestone: An unusual iron grave slab, placed by Henry Bell, honours Robert Bain (1788 – 1827), commander of the first and second Comet steam ships. The inscription provides a fascinating piece of maritime history: *"....the Comet Steam Boat in 1814, by which Vessel a communication was opened up between the Western Islands of Scotland and Glasgow, through the Crinan Canal in July 1819.*

Robert Bain's Gravestone

He was the first Captain who commanded a Vessel from Sea to Sea, through the great Caledonian Canal, in 1822."

Rosslea Hall Hotel, built in 1849 as the country house of a wealthy Victorian businessman, retains its original charm and character whilst offering superb accommodation and dining in either the award winning Garden Rooms Restaurant or the Glen Fruin Bar. Within the grounds is a plaque to Clan McAulay.

The Royal Northern & Clyde Yacht Club, established in 1824, has a clubhouse, moorings and an RYA training centre. The club owns a collection of historic yacht half models. Temporary membership available to visiting yachtsmen/women from other sailing clubs.

Shandon

Shandon, with its pleasant shingle beach, once had a pier and was another fashionable location for wealthy businessmen who had made their fortunes "across the water". Robert Napier, the ship builder, had a house here.

Blacks Livery Stables offer pony trekking. Pre-booking necessary. Tel: 01436 820838.

Shandon Country Pursuits is a centre for clay pigeon shooting, archery and off road driving amidst glorious countryside overlooking Gareloch. Pre-booking necessary. Tel: 01436 820838.

Faslane has long been a base for submarines, including steam driven ones as long ago as WW1. Its presence is evident from the miles of land bordered with razor wire and security warnings.

Glen Fruin: A minor road heads off east from near Faslane into Glen Fruin.

Garelochhead

With the arrival of steam passenger ferries and then, in 1894, the railway, this once remote village became accessible, for holidays and as a place from which to commute to Glasgow. It is a friendly and welcoming place, with an inn, pharmacy, police station, medical centre, convenience store, a choice of cafés and several B and Bs. It is a popular destination for visiting yachts.

Garelochhead Station is on the scenic West Highland Line from Glasgow to Oban Fort William and Mallaig.

The Anchor Inn is a traditional inn in the centre of the village with cosy log fires and an extensive range of malt whiskies to keep out the chill! Food served every day, pool table, satellite football, live music on Saturdays. Free moorings for visiting boats.

The Post Office has a cash machine and sells groceries, newspapers, postcards stationery, lottery tickets and a good selection of greetings cards.

Eureka Store appears to sell just about everything from hardware to all those bits and bobs which are usually difficult to find when away from home, including tent pegs, fresh flowers, fishing tackle and calor gas.

Café Craft is a café and craft shop selling yarn, haberdashery and hand-made items including felt bags, personalised cushions and unusual jewellery made from recycled glass from the shore.

Shore Road: A path follows the head of Gareloch - a pleasant stroll with panoramic views down the loch as well as a glimpse of the extent of MOD installations in the area.

Autopoint Fastfit offer auto repairs, exhausts, tyres and a breakdown recovery service. Tel: 01436 811111

Garelochhead Parish Church, built in 1837 with later extensions, is a tall and impressive white-painted building. By the gate is a cross salvaged from St. Margaret's Church, Rosyth, intertwined with an anchor crafted by Royal Navy engineers.

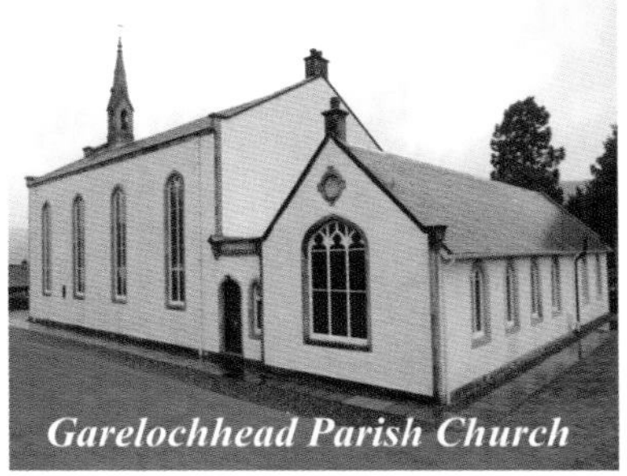

Garelochhead Parish Church

Centre 81 is a super welcoming place with an indoor climbing wall, table tennis, internet access, a café (serving hot lunches & home baking), takeaway service, canoe & kayak hire (also waterproofs & wetsuits), B and B and hostel accommodation. A children's colouring corner keeps small people busy while grown-ups enjoy a peaceful cup of coffee. Open all year.

From Garelochhead, the B833 runs south to Rosneath and on to Kilcreggan, the road shaded by beech and sycamore trees and, in places, lined with rhododendrons. The Rosneath Peninsula, known locally as "The Green Isle", is a leisurely place to explore with "olde worlde" charm, spectacular views over Gareloch, Loch Long and the Clyde and place names which proclaim "welcome".

THE ROSNEATH PENINSULA

Isabella Campbell Memorial, signposted a few hundred yards south of the B872/B833 junction, remembers an exceptionally pious 19th century woman whom many think should have been declared a saint. Near a waterfall is a small enclosure, sheltered by an oak tree. A plaque bears the inscription "Here Isabella Campbell was wont to pray." Nearby are a picnic table and seats. The path continues for a longer walk.

Isabella Campbell Memorial

Clynder is a small hamlet, behind which the hills are particularly profuse in a nectar-producing heather. At one time the area was divided into "apiaries" - small parcels of land used by bee-keepers who paid their rent in honey. From 1866 the village had a pier and Clyde paddle steamers operated until the early 1940s. Moses McNeil, founder of Rangers Football Club, lived at Clynder until his death in 1938.
Clynder Stores is a general store, newsagent and calor gas stockist. Open daily 07.00 – 20.00.

Rosneath

A settlement has probably existed here since around 600AD when Saint Modan (also known as Saint Meriden) established a monastery. The name "Rosneath" may derive from the Gaelic "Rosneimhidh" meaning "sanctuary" or "Rossnachoich" ("Virgin's headland") or "Ross-neoth" (a headland bare of trees). A pier was built here in 1893. During WWII Rosneath had a large naval base. The village has a Co-operative supermarket, post office, butcher, primary school and two churches.
The Clachan is an interesting little street with traditional cottages, one of which was the smithy. The original post box can be seen in the wall of the former post office.
St. Gilda's RC Church is a large, modern church, completed in 1968 and said to resemble the prow of a ship facing the loch. St. Gilda was born on the Clyde but travelled widely in Wales, France and Ireland before living as a hermit on an island in the Bristol Channel. There, he wrote a scholarly book entitled "De Excidio Britanniae" about the Roman occupation of Britain. He is thought to have returned to Brittany where he founded a monastery.
St. Modan's Parish Church (1853) was designed by David Cousin and stands in the grounds of an earlier church, the bell from which is displayed inside the newer building and which was rung to rally men to fight during the 1715 Jacobite Uprising. Also in the church is a carved stone, thought to be the 6th century gravestone of St. Modan. Outside, two original chapel walls remain, complete with memorial slabs. One honours Sir James MacNabb who died in India in 1846 and is remembered for "the noble example set by him during the great plague in Bombay which led to his premature and deeply lamented death." Ancient gravestones behind the present church bear some poignant inscriptions. As was normal practice, the text sometimes continues to the end of the stone, even if splitting a word or name between two lines!

Chapel Ruins

Rosneath Castle once stood at Rosneath Point. Over the centuries several castles were built and destroyed here, the last erected in 1803 for the Duke of Argyll. During WWII American troops were based at the castle. It was later demolished.
Rosneath Castle Park is a loch-side holiday park in the grounds of the former castle. There is a licensed café/bistro, well stocked shop, water activities centre and woodland walks. Non residents are welcome to walk in the grounds.

Castle Isle Restaurant/Bar in Rosneath Castle Park serves freshly prepared "pub grub" using local meat and welcomes non residents. Open daily till late. (seasonal)

Kilcreggan

Kilcreggan has the feeling of not quite having kept pace with changes elsewhere. The village developed during Victorian times and is still remarkably well serviced for a place of its size: There is a butcher, bank, barber, café, hotel, well stocked convenience store, public conveniences and probably the smallest branch in Britain of a well known chemist!

Kilcreggan Pier, built in 1897, is the Clyde's last working traditional wooden pier, looking much as it did to Victorian travellers. A frequent passenger ferry operates to Gourock.

Kilcreggan Pier

Picnic Area: Overlooking the pier, the picnic tables and seats here are a particularly nice place to watch the World go by.

The Lighthouse is a lounge bar with Sky Sports TV and a venue for live music.

The Café at Kilcreggan is a licensed café/ restaurant, serving home-cooked meals, seafood, speciality teas and coffees, home-made cakes and priding itself on good old fashioned Scottish hospitality. On the walls is a collection of iconic Norman Wilson railway posters.

K. Walker's is a superb, family run butcher's shop, selling home-made beefburgers, sausages & steak pies, as well as locally grazed lamb. A speciality (great for self catering visitors) is Kevin's Mum's range of ready-to-cook curries and casseroles.

Kevin Walker, Butcher

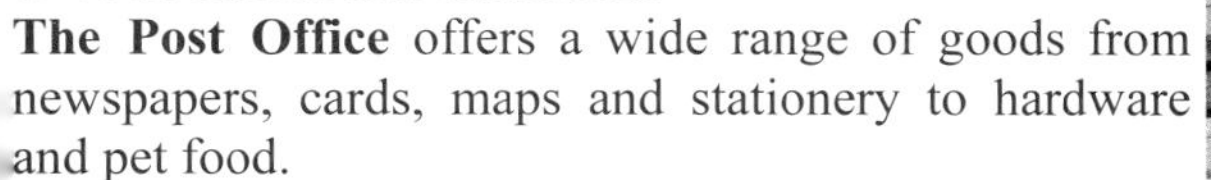

The Post Office offers a wide range of goods from newspapers, cards, maps and stationery to hardware and pet food.

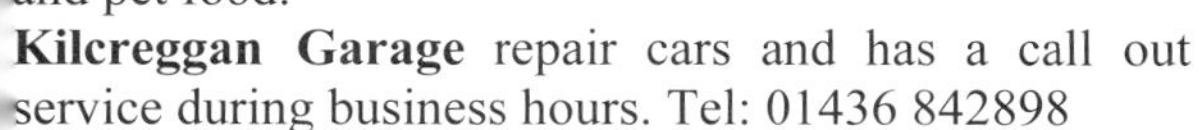

Kilcreggan Garage repair cars and has a call out service during business hours. Tel: 01436 842898

The Kilcreggan Hotel is a friendly, family run hotel which enjoys stunning views over the Clyde and has a reputation for its home-made sticky toffee pudding and chocolate cake! Lunch and dinner served daily. Open all year.

The Tut Tut Rock

From Kilcreggan the road to Cove meanders along a shoreline of shingle and rocky beaches and elegant Victorian mansions. There are seats and several picnic areas.

The Tut Tut Rock: On the shore, midway between Kilcreggan and Cove, a large rock closely resembling a head has been painted to enhance the illusion.

Cove

Cove is a small village with a convenience store and post office but also some remarkable architecture. Cove and Kilcreggan were orginally owned by the 8th Duke of Argyll. In the mid 1850s the Duke, in need of money, sold several large plots of land to prosperous Clyde businessmen who built mansions and castles as holiday homes.

Cove Burgh Hall & Reading Rooms: In 1865 Cove and Kilcreggan became a burgh with a provost and burgh hall, completed in 1893. It is an impressive, red sandstone building with a library and gathering rooms where Allied troops were entertained during WWII. When the council decided to close the hall, the community bought the property for £1. It now hosts community events and amateur dramatics. Inside are the original burgh seal and the provost's spade.

Cove Burgh Hall

Craigrownie Castle, now an exclusive rental property, was built in 1852 by architect Alexander 'Greek' Thomson.

Craigrownie Parish Church, signposted from the main road, dates from the 1850s and has an attractive interior. Its cruciform design (cross-shaped) is that of architect David Cousin. It was later enlarged by Honeyman and Keppie, with whom Charles Rennie Mackintosh had associations. Open by arrangement. Tel: 01436 842184

The War Memorial, opposite the Burgh Hall, is an elegantly sculpted Celtic cross in memory of Cove and Kilcreggan men who died in the two World Wars.

Linn Botanic Gardens: More than simply a designed landscape surrounding a mid 19th century villa, this is a true botanic garden. Collections of carefully nurtured plants from all over the World are labelled and catalogued for reference. Notable are preserved rare native species such as British balsam (not the invasive Himalayan balsam seen on riverbanks throughout the UK). The extensive grounds are a delight with rockeries, ponds, lily beds, a bamboo garden and a glen down which tumbles the Meikle Burn and which is home to spectacular ferns and a glorious collection of exotic Rhododendrons. Open daily 11.00. – 17.00.

Linn Botanic Gardens

Knockderry Castle, privately owned, is an imposing building, built around 1855 and once owned by the Templetons, well known Glasgow carpet makers. During WWII it was a hospital. I the grounds are said to be the ruins of a Viking fort.

The Knockderry House Hotel was designed by architect William Leiper for wealthy Glasgow cotton merchant. In true Victorian "Baronial" style it has man turrets. The hotel is family owned and run and offers a taste of life in a countr mansion.

Beyond Ardpeaton (a popular place for herons) is Coulport, an MOD establishmen The public road veers off through woodland back towards Garelochhead.

Loch Long

Like most Clyde sea lochs, Loch Long was scoured out by glaciers millions of years ago. Its name may derive from sixty Viking long boats which arrived here in 1263 and were then dragged across the narrow strip of land dividing Lochs Long and Lomond in King Haakon's final bid to gain supremacy over the Scottish king and clan chiefs. From 1912 to 1986 torpedoes from the Greenock factory were test-fired down Loch Long into a net stretched across the water. The upper western side of Loch Long is dense woodland with many forest tracks but no roads. On the eastern shore, the A814 runs for 12 km/7.5 miles between Garelochhead and Arrochar. It is a quiet, scenic road although much is part of a military training area. There are spectacular views over the loch and north to the Arrochar Alps with many fine mature oaks along this stretch of road, interspersed with silver birch and rowan trees which are in their full glory at the end of August.

The Three Lochs Way long distance path is 54 km/34 miles long, part of it running to the east of the A814 between Garelochhead and Arrochar, criss-crossing the West Highland Railway as it does.

The Green Kettle, marked by a large wayside green kettle, is an atmospheric, traditional Scottish tea room, built as such in 1904 and still serving teas, coffees and light meals. There is also an interesting bric-a-brac shop within. Open 09.00. – 17.00. Mar. – Oct. B and B accommodation available.

Portincaple, to the west of the main road, was originally a fishing village. It was also where cattle on the drove route south were brought ashore.

Finnart Oil Terminal: The road dips to the shore to pass this huge ocean terminal which is connected to the Grangemouth oil refinery by two 93 km/58 mile pipelines. The facility was built here during WWII, protected from enemy submarines by the Clyde booms. It occupies the former Finart and Ardarroch estates. An estate lodge can still be seen and rhododendrons line the road - a common feature of estate boundaries.

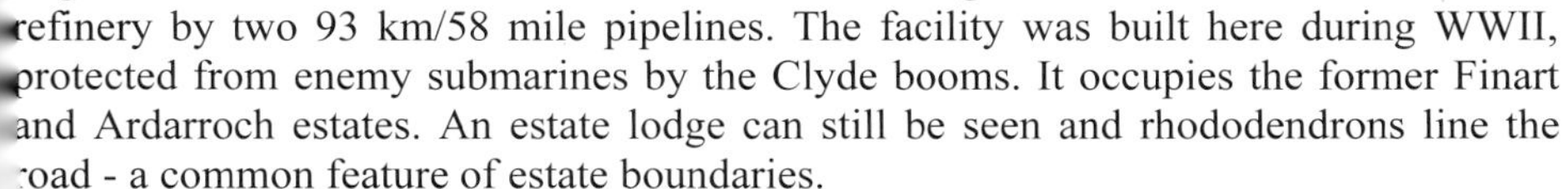

Glen Douglas: A minor road runs from the A814, through Glen Douglas to Inverbeg on Loch Lomond. Alternatively, a gated track leaves the minor road and heads north to Tarbet.

Morelaggan: 4 km/2.5 miles south west of Arrochar the road passes through this tiny hamlet, above which is High Morelaggan, a deserted "ferm toun" (collection of farm buildings) which was occupied for several hundred years until the early 20th century.

The Head of Loch Long

INDEX

Anchor Inn	16	Kidston Park	6
Ardardan Estate	11	Kilcreggan	**19**
Ardencaple Hotel	14	Kilcreggan Hotel	19
Ardmore Point	11	Kilmahew Castle	14
Baptist Church	10	Knochderry Castle	20
Blacks Livery Stables	16	Knockderry House Hotel	20
Bombed Church	13	Lifeboat Station	15
Café Craft	17	Linn Botanic Gardens	20
Cardross	**12 - 14**	Loch Long	**21**
Cardross Golf Club	13	Moore's Bridge	13
Cardross Parish Church	12	Morelaggan	21
Centenary Crosses	9	Old Police Office	8
Clynder	**18**	Portincaple	21
Colquhoun Square	**9**	Provost Lamps	7
Comet	5	Queen's Hotel	7
Comet Flywheel	7	Rhu	**14 - 16**
Coulport	20	Rhu & Shandon Church	15
Cove	**20**	Rhu Inn	15
Cove Burgh Hall	20	Rhu Marina	14
Craigendoran	**11**	Robert Bain's Grave	15 -16
Craigrownie Castle	20	Rosneath	**18 - 19**
Craigrownie Church	20	Rosneath Castle Park	18
East Esplanade	6-7	Rosneath Peninsula	**17 - 20**
Faslane	5	Rowan Gallery	6
Garelochhead	**16 - 17**	Shandon	**16**
Garelochhead Church	17	Shandon Country Pursuits	16
Geilston Gardens	12	Sir James Colquhoun	5
Glen Douglas	21	St. Andrew's Kirk	9
Glenarn Gardens	15	St. Columba's Church	8
Green Kettle	21	St. Gilda's Church	18
Helensburgh	**1 -11**	St. Mahew's Chapel	12
Helensburgh Cat	8	St. Michael & All Angels	9
Helensburgh Golf Club	10	St. Modan's Church	18
Henry Bell	5, **6,** 8, 15	St. Peter's seminary	14
Heritage Room	8	The Coach House Inn	13
Hermitage Park	10	Three Lochs Way	21
High Morelaggan	21	Tut Tut Rock	19
Hill House	10	Victoria Halls	10
Imperial Hotel	6	Visit Scotland	5
Isabella Campbell	17	West Esplanade	5-7
John Logie Baird	5, 6, **7**	Yacht Club	16

Helensburgh Library & Heritage Centre

In partnership with Helensburgh Heritage Trust

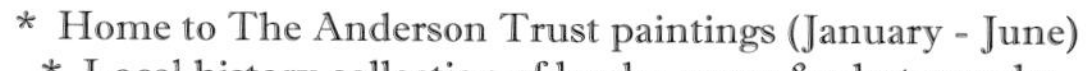

* Home to The Anderson Trust paintings (January - June)
* Local history collection of books, maps & photographs
* Collection of local newspapers dating back to first editions
* Internet access * Story telling

Many artefacts of local interest on display including....
* John Logie Baird's first "televisor"
* Painting of J.L. Baird by Steve Conroy
* Boar War Carriage Clock
* Collection of Mauchline Ware

Also on display....
Model of Henry Bell's
Comet 1

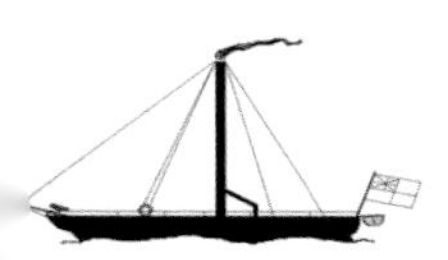

Opening times
Mon: 13.00 - 20.00. Tue/Wed: 09.30 - 13.00. 14.00 - 17.00. Thur: 13.00 - 20.00
Fri: 13.00 - 17.00. Sat: 09.30 - 13.00. 14.00 - 17.00
Tel: 01436 658833. Email: helensburghlibrary@agyll-bute.gov.uk

USEFUL TELEPHONE NUMBERS

For Police, Fire, Ambulance, Mountain Rescue, Coastguard, Tel: 999 (or 112)

olice Offices are located at Helensburgh and Garelochhead. Non-emergency, Tel: 101
HS 24: Tel: 08454 242424 (Subject to possible change)
ospital: Victoria Infirmary, Helensburgh. (A & E 08.00 - 20.00) Tel: 01436 672158
elensburgh Medical Centre: East King Street. Tel: 01436 672277/673366
entists: Dunlop & Humphreys. Tel: 01436 673197. Helensburgh Dental Practice. Tel: 436 673856. Michael Hamill. Tel: 01436 673660. H. Sweeney. Tel: 01436 674050
harmacies: Boots The Chemist, Sinclair Street, Helensburgh; Central Pharmacy, West inces Street, Helensburgh; MacNabs Pharmacy, West Princes Street, Helensburgh; oss Chemists, Sinclair Street, Helensburgh; Sinclairs, Garelochhead; Boots The emist, Kilcreggan.
ets: Lomond Veterinary Clinic, Suffolk Street, Helensburgh. Tel: 01436 676752 rklea Vetinerary Surgery, East King Street, Helensburgh. Tel: 01436 672558
hour Breakdown Service: Andrew's Garage Services, East king Street, lensburgh. Tel: 01436 646675; Fast Fit, Main Street, Helensburgh. Tel: 01436 7778
eakdown Service (daytime): Autopoint Fastfit, Garelochhead. Tel: 01436 811111

e publishers would like to thank all those who have so generously contributed their e and local knowledge towards this book, especially Donald Fullerton of lensburgh and The Helensburgh Heritage Trust. (www.helensburgh-heritage.co.uk) e publishers would also like to acknowledge help received from Argyll and Bute uncil, The National Trust for Scotland, Visit Scotland and the staff of The Forestry mmission, Historic Scotland and other organisations.

SEE IT, DO IT, DON'T MISS IT....."

The guide book series which helps visitors to do just that!

SKYE & LOCHALSH: THE GUIDE BOOK. (SECOND EDITION)
ISBN: 978-0-9562126-5-8 (64 pages)

FORT WILLIAM & THE ROAD TO THE ISLES: THE GUIDE BOOK.
ISBN 978-0-9562126-2-7 (68 pages)

AROUND LOCH NESS: THE GUIDE BOOK.
ISBN: 978-0-9562126-1-0 (64 pages)

COWAL & BUTE: THE GUIDE BOOK.
ISBN 978-0-9562126-6-5 (80 pages)

HELENSBURGH & THE ROSNEATH PENINSULA: THE GUIDE BOOK.
ISBN 978-0-9562126-7-2 (24 pages)

LOCH LOMOND & THE TROSSACHS: THE GUIDE BOOK.
ISBN 978-0-9562126-3-4 (72 pages)

Each book includes:

- All the major attractions plus many lesser known places
- Location maps - Local knowledge - Folklore & history
- Index for easy reference - Useful telephone numbers

The "See it, Do it, Don't Miss It....." series of guide books are handy, informative and packed from cover to cover with things to see and do. There are endless booklets and leaflets, many of them free, which advertise the major tourist attractions but what these books offer in addition is to take the visitor on a far more intimate tour. All our books are full of local knowledge, including all the main attractions but also travelling "off the beaten track," explaining what is to be seen, dipping into folklore and legend and discovering all sorts of delights along the way - fascinating cairns and memorials, quirky roadside features, small and remote craft studios, unique galleries, abandoned villages, ruined castles with murky histories and much, much more.

Each book is arranged in a logical order for touring either part or all of an area and is further divided into sections, each having its own map of attractions and points of interest.

Aird Trading (Publishing)

ALSO:

HAGGIS: THE RECIPE BOOK
ISBN 978-0-9562126-4-1 (32 pages)

www.scotlandbooks.co.uk
www.scotlandguidebooks.co.uk